CATHOLICISM IN
UXBRIDGE

Nicholas Schofield

CATHOLICISM IN
UXBRIDGE
A Brief History

ST PAULS

Cover design: C. González, ssp.
Cover picture: Exterior of church in 1931 and 2011

ST PAULS Publishing
187 Battersea Bridge Road, London SW11 3AS, UK
www.stpaulspublishing.com

ISBN: 978-0-85439-825-6

A catalogue record is available
for this book from the British Library.

Set by C. González, ssp.
Printed by Bishops Printers, Portsmouth, UK.

ST PAULS is an activity of the priests and brothers
of the Society of St Paul who proclaim the Gospel
through the media of social communication.

CONTENTS

PREFACE

EVERY parish has a story. Although this is often hidden from most parishioners, only a little effort is required to uncover it and there are always surprises along the way.

This short history is based largely on sources held in the parish and diocesan archives, as well as memories and photos kindly supplied by parishioners. The local studies section in the local library also proved most helpful, as did that doyen of Uxbridge historians, Ken Pearce, and Sr Rosemary, who provided invaluable information regarding Pield Heath.

On the surface, a parish history may seem to be mainly a tale of building work, fundraising and the occasional special event. Some may think it is a narrative largely based around bishops and priests. But something much deeper – or should we say someone – is truly at work.

The famous preacher Mgr Ronald Knox once observed that wars and social developments were only the 'backwash on the current' of history; what really mattered was an individual's journey to God. Any parish church is 'a great museum of unwritten history,' he said, 'the history that really counts'.

This book was written as part of the celebrations marking the present church's eightieth birthday, in gratitude to all the priests and people who have worked in the Uxbridge area, stretching back into the mists of time.

Fr Nicholas Schofield
Parish Priest

Uxbridge
15 May 2011

THE CHURCH
IN MEDIEVAL UXBRIDGE

THE ORIGINS of Christianity in the Uxbridge area go back over a millennium and a half. Perhaps the earliest relic of the Faith is to be found in Cowley. An excavation in 1965 revealed part of a Roman road that may have eventually led to Verulamium (St Albans). It has been suggested that the church of St Lawrence was built beside this ancient highway on the site of a Roman temple, perhaps shortly after the arrival of St Augustine of Canterbury and his monks (597) or even earlier. This would account for the rather strange location of the church, away from the village centre.

During better-documented times, local land was owned by prominent medieval religious houses. Cowley Peachey belonged to the Benedictine monks of Westminster Abbey and part of the manor of Colham was granted to Evesham Abbey in Worcestershire, which also exercised patronage over the parish of Hillingdon. Moreover, Bishopshalt School reminds us that the bishops of Worcester once owned a house in the area where they could stay while travelling to and from London, where they had a house just off the Strand.

Uxbridge itself was originally part of the parish of Hillingdon. By the thirteenth century there was a chapel of ease at Uxbridge dedicated to St Margaret of Antioch, the popular virgin martyr who, according to legend, was once swallowed by a dragon (the devil in disguise) but was spat out when the cross she carried irritated the beast's stomach. It is intriguing that the two patrons of the current Catholic parish in Uxbridge are also often depicted triumphing over evil in the same way: Our Lady of Lourdes, shown trampling on the serpent, and St Michael, the heavenly warrior defeating Satan.

Despite not being a parish in its own right until the nineteenth century, Uxbridge became an important commercial centre. In 1239 Henry III granted a yearly fair in the town on 'the Vigil, the Feast and the Morrow of St Margaret'. From the 1290s there were further fairs held on the feasts of St Michael (29 September) and St Nicholas (6 December), as well as a weekly market.

St Margaret's church appears to have been largely rebuilt in the early fifteenth century. Later in the century the south aisle was added for the use of the Guild of St Mary and St Margaret, which had been founded in 1448. Many parishes before the Reformation had these highly active lay organisations, which took on a variety of roles – prayer group (by providing Masses or candles at a particular altar), charity, social club, trade union, local government agency and bank. The Uxbridge Guild provided for a chaplain 'to celebrate Divine Service in the same Chapel for the good estate of the King and Queen and the members of the Guild and for their Souls after death, and the souls of the King's parents and progenitors'. There were also two elected chapelwardens and the guild came to own property in the town. In 1548 the possessions of the guild, including land in Cowley Field, the George Inn, and shops and houses in Uxbridge, were worth £11.

A chantry for the soul of Walter Shiryngton, Chancellor of the Duchy of Lancaster, was endowed in 1459 with 27 acres of land and tenements in the town. By 1470 Eton College was the patron of the chantry. A priest was employed 'for the daily celebration of divine Mass at the altar of the Blessed Virgin Mary in St Margaret's Chapel' as well as attending vespers on holy days and the 'singing of the anthem *Ave Maria* in his surplice' and 'to say every week the *Placebo* and *Dirige* with nine lessons for the souls of brothers and sisters, living and dead, of the Guild or Fraternity of the Blessed Virgin Mary in Uxbridge'.

The late medieval Church was full of vitality. There were new devotions, such as the cult centred around the unfortunate Henry VI, murdered in 1471 during the Wars of the Roses. If his leadership was often put into question, he was widely recognised for his piety and many pilgrims flocked to his shrine at St George's Chapel in Windsor Castle. Perhaps some of them passed through Uxbridge. Another popular devotion, never officially recognised by the authorities, was centred on 'St' Thomas of Lancaster, beheaded for his opposition to Edward II in 1322. Shrines to him appeared all over the country, including an image at Hillingdon. As late as 1526 a will requested burial 'before Saint Thomas of Lancaster at Hillingdon'.

HIDING HOLES
AND MARTYRS

ALMOST without warning, this vibrant, colourful world of Catholic England collapsed within the space of a few decades. Thousands of books have been written about the Protestant Reformation and there is no space here to deal with it in great detail. Suffice to say that its impact was revolutionary – splitting Christendom into 'Catholic' and 'Protestant' camps, which were as often connected to politics as to personal faith. The Faith of the King was the Faith of the nation, which is why Henry VIII's personal difficulties with his marriage to Catherine of Aragon were able to disrupt the course of history. As is well known, the pope upheld the dignity of the sacrament of marriage and refused to grant Henry his much-desired annulment. The king remained stubborn and, spurred on by his reformist advisers, the Church of England was born. Henry became Supreme Head of the English Church and effectively granted himself the much needed divorce. The break with Rome, and with it over a millennium of tradition, involved the gradual destruction of vestiges of the 'old religion', such as the monasteries and shrines.

There is little evidence of the immediate impact of the Reformation in Uxbridge. At first little really changed on the local level. The English were used to battles between the King and the Church; wise men hoped that things would one day sort themselves out. There was much uncertainty as each of Henry's children pursued a very different policy – the reign of Edward VI saw the continued destruction of Catholic England; his sister, Mary, restored England to the old Faith but died before it could be consolidated; and Elizabeth continued the path of her father, in which the monarch always knew best.

During the reign of Mary Uxbridge was the unhappy location of the burning of three Protestants: John Denley, Robert Smith and Patrick Packingham (or Rockingham), all of whom suffered at the Lynch Green in August 1555. None were local men – Denley was from Maidstone and Smith had worked at Eton College - but they were brought to Uxbridge since it was an important commercial centre and their death could act as a deterrent.

Denley's execution, on 8 August, became particularly celebrated in the collective memory thanks to the vivid description found in John Foxe's *Book of Martyrs.* We read that

> while suffering in agony, and singing a psalm, Dr Story inhumanly ordered one of the tormentors to throw a fagot at him, which cut his face severely, caused him to cease singing, and to raise his hands to his face. Just as Dr Story was remarking in jest that he had spoiled a good song, the pious martyr again chanted, spread his hands abroad m the flames, and through Christ Jesus resigned his soul into the hands of his Maker'.

Foxe was writing as a martyrologist rather than a historian, eager to honour the memory of those who suffered and show the perceived savagery of Catholicism. Interestingly, 'cruel Dr Story' was eventually captured and condemned to death under the regime of Elizabeth. His execution proceeded with great severity on 1 June 1571 and he was later beatified as a Catholic martyr by Pope Leo XIII.

These were very different times from our own, when personal creed was seen as a matter affecting the stability of the state and heresy the worst of crimes. Moreover, executions were common and served as popular entertainment as well as a carefully scripted 'theatre of justice' that could be used to the advantage of both persecutor and persecuted. As Eamon Duffy writes in his study of Catholic England under Mary Tudor, *Fires of Faith:*

> For the bishops, it was an opportunity to recall straying sheep to the unity of the church, to correct their errors and to set out authentic catholic teaching. And, since much of the examination, and invariably its final stage, was carried out before spectators in open court, it was also a public performance, a solemn piece of theatre in which justice was displayed. In London especially, it was an opportunity to demonstrate to a sometimes hostile lay audience that every effort was being made to win the accused over by persuasion...For the accused, it was of course a tribunal with powers of life and death, a terrifying ordeal that, if they remained faithful to their convictions, could only end in an appalling and painful death. But it was also an evangelical opportunity to witness against the errors of antichrist, to vindicate their own fidelity to the Gospel, to prove the bloodthirsty cruelty of the bishops and to persuade the onlookers to embrace the protestant cause.

Jesuits at Uxbridge

Uxbridge became an important centre of Catholicism during the reign of Elizabeth. 'Southlands', the house of William Griffiths on the Denham road, was used for the famous meeting of English Jesuits in October 1580.

This is probably the same property that was used briefly by ten members of the Bridgettine community of Syon Abbey after the dissolution of the monasteries in the 1530s. Visitors to the Anglican church at Denham can still see a relic of their short sojourn in the fine brass showing Abbess Agnes Jordan, Syon's last pre-Reformation superior.

In October and November 1580 St Edmund Campion, Fr Robert Persons and other Jesuits gathered at Southlands for a conference. They had had a similar meeting at Hoxton, in east London, that July but it was now considered unsafe for them be too close to the city. 'Jesuits and Massing priests' were increasingly wanted men, especially after the recent publication of Campion's *Brag (or Challenge to the Privy Council)*, a bold defense of Catholicism.

At Southlands reports were made of the Fathers' progress so far. Their mission in England had only begun the previous year. Campion spoke of his work in Berkshire, Northamptonshire and Oxfordshire and the converts he had made, including Lord Vaux of Harrowden, Sir William Catesby (who owned property in Uxbridge, as we shall see) and Sir Thomas Tresham. A number of important decisions were then made for the immediate future: Fr Persons would remain in the London area while Campion would go to Lancashire, a traditional stronghold of Ca-

**Fr Robert Persons, one of the Jesuits
who met in Uxbridge during October 1580**

tholicism and a safe distance from the capital. He would also write a polemical work in Latin directed at the Universities of Oxford and Cambridge - the celebrated *Rationes Decem* (Ten Reasons). Two other Jesuits who seem to have been present at the Uxbridge Conference, William Hartley and Arthur Pitts, were sent to the Universities to help those who wanted to embrace the Faith and perhaps enter one of the foreign seminaries.

Another consequence of the meeting was the establishment of clandestine printing presses at Greenstreet, East Ham and then Stonor Park, Oxfordshire. The Welsh priest Robert Gwyn was present at the meeting and went on to set up a press in a coastal cave near Llandudno in 1586–7, where part of *Y drych Kristnogawl* (probably written by Gwyn) was produced. This work was the first Welsh language book to be printed in Wales.

Campion and Persons resolved to report back to the Father General of the Jesuits in Rome and, after prayer, discussion, confession and renewal of vows, the Jesuits parted company, each committing 'his fellow to the grace of Almighty God, with the tenderness of heart which in such a case and so dangerous a time may be imagined, when they might hardly hope to see ever the one the other again'. Indeed, Campion would be captured and martyred on

1 December 1581. Today, his relics return to Uxbridge each year, as part of an annual pilgrimage organised by the Knights of St Columba, tracing the journey from the place of his capture, Lyford Grange, to the place of his martyrdom at Tyburn.

Another centre of Elizabethan Catholicism near Uxbridge was Morecrofts, or Moorcroft, a name still found locally ('Moorcroft Lane', 'Moorcroft Park'), which belonged to Sir William Catesby and then his son Robert (one of the gunpowder plotters). It was briefly used as the headquarters of Fr Henry Garnet, the Jesuit superior in England. According to Jesuit historian Philip Caraman, 'it was sufficiently near the city to provide a convenient refuge for incoming priests, yet remote enough to escape organized searches that were confined to the capital'. Among others, the mother of Fr Persons was given shelter there, often described in correspondence as 'the old woman'. After the dramatic escape of the Jesuit John Gerard from the Tower on 4 October 1597, he rode to Uxbridge with St Nicholas Owen ('Little John'). They had dinner with Fr Garnet and 'the rejoicing was great. We all thanked God that I had escaped from the hands of my enemies in the name of the Lord'.

The following March the Jesuit Oswald Tesimond arrived in England with Ralph Ashley and visited Morecrofts where 'we were received with the warmest welcome and the greatest charity imaginable.' Several days after, word arrived from London that 'the Privy Council had had notice of that house and that without doubt the Queen's officers would come to search it that very night.' Tesimond was impressed by Garnet's great calm, proving himself 'to be an old soldier and experienced captain, accustomed to such assaults.' Garnet 'gave orders to hide in the hiding-places which had long since been prepared for such an occurrence, everything that could show that the house belonged to Catholics: as books, altar vestments, pictures and everything of the sort; and then stowed away all things of greater value.' Tesimond and Ashley were then sent away and told to await Garnet at Brentford, to be taken to 'another house he had in London, which he kept on purpose to be able to retire to it in similar emergencies'. According to the historian of Hillingdon, Rachel de Salis, 'there is a fairly well authenticated tradition that ten priests were hidden for four days in a secret place in the house, the floor of which was several inches deep in water'.

Jesuits were also active in Denham, just outside Uxbridge, in the mid-1580s. Under the leadership of Fr William Weston, a group of priests (including the future martyr Blessed

John Cornelius) celebrated a number of public exorcisms to prove to the people the power of the Catholic Faith. Denham was the epicentre of this rather unusual form of evangelisation, but another location was the house in Uxbridge of a certain 'Hughes'. The exorcisms were sensationally reported in a book by the anti-Catholic Samuel Harsnett and the various names given for the devil inspired Shakespeare for a scene in *King Lear*, where Edgar says:

> Five fiends have been in poor Tom at once; of lust, as Obidicut; Hobbididance, prince of dumbness; Mahu, of stealing; Modo, of murder; Flibbertigibbet, of mobbing and mowing; who since possesses chambermaids and waiting-women (IV, i).

There were other local centres of recusancy. Thomas Paget, the fourth Baron Paget, lived at West Drayton Manor and was a well-known 'papist'. In 1581 a government agent alleged that the great composer, William Byrd – himself a Catholic and a resident of nearby Harlington – could often be found at 'the Lord Padgettes house Draighton'. The following year spies reported that Lady Paget was giving money for the relief of priests in prison and that a priest lived at West Drayton as a steward. Lord Paget himself had to escape to France in 1583 because of his support for Mary, Queen of Scots.

'SECOND SPRING'

THERE IS little evidence regarding Uxbridge Catholics in the seventeenth and eighteenth centuries. One could mention Henry Bennet, first earl of Arlington, a convert to the Catholic Faith who acted as Secretary of State to Charles II. His family owned land locally, including the Crown and Treaty House in Uxbridge. Another fleeting Catholic presence was provided by Irish members of James II's disbanded army, who passed through Uxbridge and behaved rather badly.

In 1706 two papists, one living in Uxbridge and the other in Hillingdon parish, are mentioned in a parochial return. Then there is hardly a mention of Catholicism until 1812, when the body of Lady Mary Elizabeth Nugent, the Catholic Marchioness of Buckingham and Baroness Nugent of Carlanstown, rested in Uxbridge on its way to Stowe and

Office of the Dead was recited and a Requiem celebrated in the mortuary chapel – presumably the first Mass to be said openly in the area since the Reformation.

The modern Catholic history of Uxbridge only starts with the foundation of a Catholic 'mission' (as parishes in this country were called until 1917) at West Drayton. Mass was first celebrated in a stable behind the King's Head Inn (now 29 The Green). In 1862 Fr Andrew Mooney leased 'White Cottage' on Money Lane as a Mass centre and a temporary home for 'St Augustine's Catholic School' (the forerunner of St Catherine's). In June 1867 he was replaced by Fr Peter Francis Elkins, who wrote to the local paper:

> To the Roman Catholics (if any) of Uxbridge and its vicinity.
>
> Sir,
>
> Will you allow me to make known through your paper to all or any Catholics as above that West Drayton is erected into a mission and included Uxbridge, Iver, Cowley, Hillingdon, etc., that the priest resides at West Drayton where Catholics number over 300. They celebrate Mass on Sundays at 10am and daily at 7am with evening devotions on Sunday at 6.30, on weekdays at 8pm during the summer months.

The little chapel had room for forty people but already in August 1867 Fr Elkins reported in *The Tablet* that one Sunday '130 Catholics were counted as obliged to kneel outside,' which led him to wonder 'what are the poor Catholics to do in the depth of winter if no chapel able to shelter them be created?' Archbishop Henry Edward Manning of Westminster wrote to support his appeal: the fact that 'more than 300 Catholics would be deprived of Mass and the Holy Sacraments except by going to a distance of five miles is an abundant and evident reason for your undertaking to provide a small church in the midst of them'.

Shortly afterwards Fr Michael Aloysius Wren was appointed to the new mission. Born at Charlemont, County Armagh in 1835, he had been ordained by Manning in 1865 – the first priest to be ordained by this eminent Victorian. At West Drayton, *The Tablet* later reported that Fr Wren's 'congregation was numerous but scattered, and consisted entirely of poor immigrants who could give no material help. In the face, however, of many difficulties and under the pressure of many hardships he laboured with a zeal that never flagged and a courage that never failed. His generous and persevering efforts Almighty God has blessed and crowned. There stands today in West Drayton a monument to the life and labours of Father Wren, a beautiful church, excellent schools and a convenient presbytery'. The church was dedicated to St Catherine the Martyr at the request of Richard Swift, former Sheriff of London, who had donated £1,000 towards the cost of building and whose wife was called Catherine. It was opened by the Archbishop on 30 September 1869 and was designed by Messrs Wilson and Nicholl in the style of the fourteenth century. In subsequent years Fr Wren worked hard to pay off the £1,000 debt so that the church could be consecrated, which happy event took place at Michaelmas 1893 at the hands of Cardinal Vaughan.

**Fr John Wren, appointed in 1892
to assist his uncle (see p33)**

THE BEGINNINGS
OF THE UXBRIDGE MISSION

UXBRIDGE was originally served from West Drayton and Catholics would make the three mile walk each Sunday or catch a train from Uxbridge Vine Street. Indeed, the *Catholic Directory* even noted under the entry for St Catherine's: 'Trains from and to Uxbridge bef[ore] and aft[er] 1st M[ass] on Sun[day],' which was at 9am.

Fr Wren realised that this situation could not continue for long and that the Catholics of Uxbridge urgently needed their own mission. At Mass on Sunday 24 January 1892, just after the death of Cardinal Manning, he

> recalled to mind that he had had the privilege of being the first to receive the sacred unction of the priesthood from the venerable hands of the late prelate. He also informed his hearers that one of the last official acts of his Eminence was to sanction the opening

of a new mission at Uxbridge, and that when he first spoke of the necessity of this work to the Cardinal, he expressed his great sympathy with the project, saying with emphasis: "I rejoice to hear it, Uxbridge and Hillingdon have been in my mind for many years." And when, about three weeks ago, he saw Cardinal Manning for the last time, as it proved, his Eminence showed such a lively and personal interest in the work that he expressed a desire to be named as co-lessee in the lease of the proposed site for the new temporary church'.

The temporary corrugated iron chapel that served as the Catholic church until 1931

This deathbed interview occurred at the end of 1891, which is traditionally given as the year of the parish's foundation, although nothing happened until 1892. Fr Wren bought a presbytery on Lawn Road and a temporary church was built nearby of corrugated iron. The chapel was opened on 29 September, the Feast of St Michael, with High Mass in the presence of the new Archbishop of Westminster, Herbert Vaughan. A chalice, made in Paris, was presented for the occasion by Josephine H. Coggeshall and is still used for Mass today. Lacking facilities for a large social event, a luncheon was then held at the Town Hall. The caterer, M. Emile Bruvet (who had a business on the High Street), was described by the local paper as providing a repast of 'a most *recherché* character'. The Archbishop, who had already delivered an address in the church, spoke a few words:

> Some of the inhabitants of the neighbourhood, he said, might think the Devil had come amongst them, but he thought that instead they would find them good angels. He thought they would find Father Wren a most amiable man, and soon become good friends. It was a great thing and extremely desirable to establish these little places in the country, for if they could Catholicise the country thus, London would soon follow.

Fr Wren himself expressed his thanks for 'the great assistance that had been accorded by friends' and mentioned that 'during his 25 years' residence at West Drayton, he had received the greatest kindness both from his Catholic and non-Catholic friends, and he might conscientiously say that he had not wilfully made an enemy'. The momentous day was concluded by an evening service, at which Fr Vaughan preached.

The corrugated iron chapel remained the church for the Catholics of Uxbridge until the present building was opened in 1931. The small space was used to maximum effect with is altars, statues and flowers.

Meanwhile, negotiations were being made concerning the opening of a school. On 22 December 1893 a site on Rockingham Road was 'purchased from Mr William Fassnidge of the Cedars, Uxbridge, in the joint names of H. E. Cardinal Herbert Vaughan and Rev. Michael Wren'. The first part of 1894 was taken up with gaining approval for the plans of the buildings and confirming its status as a 'Mixed School providing school places for 88 children'. On 6 June the Foundation Stone was laid by the Cardinal and the Honourable Mrs Harriet Le Poer Trench. Her name occasionally appears in the parish registers – for example, she acted as sponsor for the girls at the first confirmation ceremony in Uxbridge in 1897. Her husband was Colonel William Le Poer Trench, son of the third Earl of Clancarty and a Justice of the Peace in Buckinghamshire. He was also a veteran of the Second Opium War (in China, 1856-60) and had been mentioned in despatches as commander of a ladder company at the capture of Canton and Nankow.

The school buildings were quickly erected by Messrs Fassnidge and Sons, of the family that had originally owned the land, and on 24 February 1895 'St Mary's Roman Catholic School' was formally opened. Under the charge of Miss Anastasia Morrissey, the school started off with small numbers – the highest attendance the first week was 15. The priest acted as 'manager' and the log book records his regular visits and inspections.

Unfortunately, the strain of establishing missions and schools led to a breakdown in Fr Wren's health. He died in March 1896 and the Requiem was celebrated by Bishop Fenton, followed by burial in St Martin's churchyard, West Drayton. Many years later, on 12 July 1965, Cardinal Heenan prayed at the grave alongside the vicar during a visit to St Catherine's, causing a memorable scene.

**The tomb of Fr Michael Wren in the graveyard
of St Martin's, West Drayton**

It should be noted that much of the day-to-day work at Uxbridge in these early years was done by the Founder's nephew, Fr John J. Wren (known to his friends as 'Jenny'). The younger Fr Wren had been ordained on 11 June 1892, having studied at St Edmund's, Ware (where he won the coveted post of Captain of the Cricket XI) and St Thomas' Seminary, Hammersmith, and came to Uxbridge immediately after his ordination. There he remained until 1895, when he returned to St Edmund's as Prefect of Studies. According to the College magazine, 'a certain, self-imposed reserve prevented the majority of the boys from getting to know his really bright and genial personality,' but with his colleagues his 'kindly and cheerful disposition, keen sense of humour and quaint power of droll phraseology dispelled all gloom and depression.' He died in 1919, at the early age of 51, while serving as Rector of Somers Town and was buried at Kensal Green.

In the mid-1890s, there was a succession of priests at Uxbridge: Fr Lionel Goodrich, Fr Wilfred Thompson and Fr James Hazell, who was actually appointed Rector in 1896. He was a convert, having been received into the Church by Mgr Thomas John Capel (popularly known as the 'Apostle to the Genteel' on account of his connections in high society), and previous to his arrival in Uxbridge had been working as Rector of Canning Town. He built on Fr Wren's pioneering work and wrote a short report on St Mary's in the summer term of 1895: 'the school is making a very fair start, in its present condition. With five standards and infants represented in a body of 20 children, it is difficult to bring it within the four corners of any scheme of Instruction.'

At his death in 1932, *The Tablet* described Fr Hazell as 'a widely-read and interesting man, [who] hardly did justice to himself by a disposition expressed in self-effacement; but to those who enjoyed his friendship and conversation he was a mine of lore, especially as to details of Catholic life in London during the past half century'.

'Dean' John Brady

In 1897 Fr Hazell moved to Holy Trinity, Brook Green and Fr John Brady arrived in his place. A Carlow man, he had been ordained as a Marist Father and had for many years been stationed at St Anne's, Underwood Road in the east end. Here he was closely involved in Cardinal Manning's League of the Cross, which promoted total abstinence. Fr Brady also worked at Goudhurst in Kent and Haywards Heath in Sussex, before seeking incardination into the Archdiocese of Westminster and serving for a time in Bow.

He would stay at Uxbridge for eighteen years and from 1908 acted as rural dean, thus becoming known as 'Dean Brady'. This involved convening regular meetings of the local deanery, which was dedicated to St Joseph and comprised the missions of Ealing, Hanwell, Hayes, North Hyde, Twyford, Uxbridge and West Drayton. This list serves as a reminder of the relatively small number of Catholic churches in the western suburbs at the time.

Under Fr Brady's guidance the newly-founded mission of Uxbridge went from strength to strength. On Passion Sunday 1897 Cardinal Vaughan paid another visit, arriving by train and walking to the church, even though a carriage was waiting for him at the station. Mass was then celebrated by Fr Brady and the Cardinal preached on 'Tell me what you love, and I will tell you what you are'. He spoke of how the saints had attained sanctity by loving Christ in His passion and 'he recommended them to pray, to study their crucifix and the gospels, and also a little treatise on the life and passion of Christ by St Alphonsus, to read it day by day and to meditate upon it'. At three in the afternoon the Cardinal returned to the little church for Confirmation. The local paper reports that 'the place was so crowded that seats were placed in the aisle to accommodate visitors and even then many were unable to obtain admission'. Finally, there was a reception in St Mary's Schools, attended by the Le Poer Trenchs, the Gilbeys and other prominent local Catholics.

The first baptismal register gives an indication of the range of Fr Brady's labours, for candidates came not only from Uxbridge but from Hillingdon, Ruislip, Hayes, Denham and Gerrards Cross. Their backgrounds also varied enormously, from members of the well-connected Gilbey family of Denham, who found godparents from the English and Spanish aristocracy, to four members of the Donovan family christened in September 1909, whose address is stated as the 'Uxbridge Union Workhouse' – an institution which the Catholic clergy ministered to, when needed, despite not receiving a salary for their troubles.

A visitation return for 1905 gives a further glimpse of Catholic life in the still-nascent mission. An average of 84 attended Mass each Sunday and although 92 children were enrolled at the school, 64 of these were not Catholic. Despite this, Mass was celebrated at the school every Thursday morning and the children led the hymn singing during one of the Sunday Masses, though it was not a *Missa cantata* (or sung Mass) as such. These were very different times, when a nominal charge of about a penny was made for seats in the church and bench rents cost 5/- or 3/-. Moreover Fr Brady complained in his report of the state of the presbytery, which had not benefitted from repairs for some time.

Fr Brady was 'a lover of all wholesome games and sports' and 'as an Irish priest, he was at home on a horse'. He was blessed with a strong constitution and, having learnt to cycle in middle age, gave younger men a good run for their money. On one occasion he managed to travel to Ireland for his mother's ninetieth birthday and return to Uxbridge in the space of three days, which was considered an impressive feat for the times. The Dean was a well-known figure, not only as a priest but, from 1904, a member of the Urban District Council. According to his obituary in the local paper:

> He was... most regular in his attendance at Council and Committees, and most active and firm in the advocacy of his own convictions on questions that arose. It has been written of Mr W. E. Gladstone that once, after due deliberation, having come to a conclusion on a serious matter, he would never revise

it unless there was some essential change in the character or circumstances of the situation that had been under review. Father Brady seemed to act on the same principle, and thus appeared iron-willed against any change of mind, even though he were one in a thousand.

Fr John Brady

FR MOLONEY
AND THE NEW CHURCH

AT THE END of 1915 Dean Brady was appointed chaplain to St Mary's orphanage, North Hyde, where he died just over a year later, aged 79. His successor at Uxbridge was Fr Thomas Moloney. Born on 23 February 1873 at Piltown, County Kilkenny, he was trained at Maynooth and ordained for the diocese of Waterford and Lismore in 1896. Soon afterwards he moved to London and worked for many years at St Margaret's, Canning Town, then part of the Archdiocese of Westminster and its second largest parish. After six years as curate he became rector – an unusual appointment since priests often had to wait until middle age before taking charge of a parish. He extended the schools, paid off the parish debt and sat on the West Ham Board of Guardians, but the weight of responsibility eventually resulted in a breakdown in health and the contraction of scarlet fever. So, in November 1915, he was transferred to Uxbridge, which was considered a lighter 'rural' charge.

However, Fr Moloney was not content to sit back and enjoy a life of semi-retirement in Uxbridge. The parish was quickly growing and by 1928 an average of 360 were attending Sunday Mass, not including those who attended the convent chapels at Pield Heath and Hillingdon Court, which brought the number up to 400. In 1917 the Royal Flying Corps

Fr Thomas Moloney

Armament and Gunnery School was established at Hillingdon House and three years later it became 1920 RAF Central Depot, Uxbridge. Fr Moloney wrote in the 1928 Visitation Return that the base had about 80 Catholics, though 'not more than about half the men stationed [there]…are ever free to come to Mass on Sundays. The remainder are on duties of various kinds'. RAF Uxbridge would be an important presence in the town until its official closure in March 2010.

Then there was the issue of church premises. It seems that, despite his many abilities, Dean Brady had let things slip in his final years at Uxbridge and a letter from the Diocesan Finanicial Secretary, Mgr Carton de Wiart, written in October 1915 revealed that 'Fr Moloney is rather dismayed at the condition of the church, which is very bad, and of the house, which is really not fit to live in.' Indeed, Fr Moloney at first took lodgings locally before buying the current presbytery, a fine Edwardian house (37 Lawn Road) which then stood on the corner of Bassett Road and Lawn Road, in February 1916 at a cost of £1,000.

The need for a new, permanent church was the next objective and for many years Fr Moloney raised funds and considered the options. In 1929 he received the Cardinal's approval to buy the old Wesleyan Chapel on New Windsor

Street, together with its fittings. This had been opened in 1848 and, built as it was in the gothic style, would have made a fine Catholic church. It was also just down the road from St Mary's school. However, this was not to be and it became instead a masonic hall, Mgr Carton de Wiart writing to Fr Moloney: 'I think the agent has not been very kind to you. Possibly he is a Freemason himself. He ought to have told you what the Freemasons offer was and given you an opportunity of offering a little more.' In 1996 the hall was converted into flats and is today called 'Newland House'.

Fr Moloney decided to build the new church behind the presbytery and managed to acquire some of the surrounding land to make the site as large as possible. The foundation stone was laid on Low Sunday 1931 by Archbishop Alban Goodier, an English Jesuit who had been Archbishop of Bombay between 1919 and 1926. About three hundred people gathered and music was provided by the parish choir of Southall. The Archbishop sprinkled the site of the new church with holy water and addressed the faithful beside a wooden cross, which had been erected on the place where the High Altar was to be built.

> There were those [he said] who said they built churches too grand for the poverty of the people. Why not spend money on institutions,

clubs, schools, etc, they were asked. [The Catholics'] answer was that nothing was good enough for God and in spite of their poverty their churches must be more and more beautiful if they could make them so. On that account they never thought they were wasting money or means. St Augustine reminded them that the church was a symbol of what was going on in the lives of individuals. Christ lived in the church but He lived more in the individual soul, and if they made the churches beautiful there was all the more reason to make their souls beautiful in Him.

With the foundation stone was placed 'a parchment giving details', a gold sovereign (donated by the Archbishop) and several pieces taken from the grotto at Lourdes.

The new church was designed by the architect, T. H. B. Scott, who designed many churches for the diocese during the period, including those at Burnt Oak, Cricklewood, Feltham, Finchley Central, Gunnersbury, Kingsbury Green, Muswell Hill, New Barnet, North Harrow, Northfields, Parsons Green, Stoke Newington, Waltham Cross and Welwyn Garden City (St Bonaventure's). The church in Uxbridge was built of brick in the Romanesque style, seating around 350.

The church was built quickly and opened by Cardinal Bourne at Michaelmas 1931. The local

The interior of the church, 1931

Advertiser and Gazette gave a detailed report of the Cardinal's words on this occasion:

> Cardinal Bourne's sermon was a passionate appeal for adoration of God to take first place in men's hearts. This theme ran through the whole of his message. It was only right, he said, that on this occasion gratitude and joy should fill the heart. But the fact that the first thing for which a church was built was for the adoration of God should never be forgotten. He asked them to pray for those who had made the building possible, and said that Father Moloney should be grateful that most of the debt was cleared by the Uxbridge population. An anonymous gift of £3,000 had been made, and that left a debt of £2,000, which would seem lessened by the fact of the existence of the church.

> The church would give greater opportunity for Catholic worship, it would be beneficial to the non-Catholic population, and – from a third point of view – it was yet another place for the worship of God. These were all good points, but the main truth was that the church was not primarily for the people, nor for the preaching of the Word of God, but for the adoration of God Himself. People were too apt to think of a church as for the service of men.

> The Cardinal spoke of the Angels. The fact of their existence, he said, should be a great comfort. Their sole occupation was the adoration

of God. They were utterly spiritual. Through them the adoration of God never ceased. When the church was empty they are there, adoring and worshipping God. This fact should be a great comfort to everyone and a great source of help. It was a very wonderful thing that did not receive sufficient thought. To think about the angels was to awaken in their own hearts the spirit of adoration of God. Some might ask what was the use of a Catholic church in a remote place with a small population. But such a church was no less a House of God than a great cathedral. The angels were always about the altar adoring God.

Still with the theme of the adoration of God, the Cardinal touched on the present position of the world. There were self-sufficient men who often set themselves up as leaders and teachers of the people, he said. They were to be avoided. They placed men on pedestals where God alone should be. "I appeal to you", concluded the Cardinal, "to strengthen your spirit of adoration. Put yourselves in the attitude of the angels. Adoration of God comes first – the rest will fall into place. That attitude makes it possible for the angels to make your lives a service".

The Tablet added that 'the Mass music, plain-chant, was conscientiously rendered by a choir of school children. Above the new church tower floated the newly designed flag of the Vatican City. The congregation present at the opening ceremony included upwards of fifty men from the R.A.F. camp in the locality, and a number of Catholics from neighbouring parishes.'

The cost of the new church was £8,600. Churches could only be consecrated once all the debt had been cleared and this typically took decades. Mgr Carton de Wiart wrote to Fr Moloney in 1931: 'You ought now to make a huge effort and storm Our Lady of Lourdes, so that you may open the Church without debt. You will then be quite fit for Paradise!' It is a testament to Fr Moloney's administrative ability that Our Lady of Lourdes and St Michael was ready to be consecrated on 14 May 1936 – thanks to fund raising, donations and the sale of the old temporary chapel to Mr Randall for £1,000. The consecration ceremony was performed by Bishop Patrick Casey of Ross, an old seminary classmate, and the complex service lasted three hours and forty minutes.

As at Canning Town, Fr Moloney did much work with the parish schools and he extended and modernised St Mary's in 1935, adding three classrooms, childrens' cloakrooms, rooms for teachers, toilets and better heating. It came to a cost of £4,000 and efforts were quickly made to raise funds through a school building fund, including Whist Drives and a collection made each Monday when pupils were asked to donate a penny or more. By 1937 a total of £1,000 had been raised.

Fr Moloney's curates included Fr Edward J. Mahoney (1915-17), who went on to study for a doctorate at Fribourg and serve as Professor of Moral Theology at St Edmund's College, Ware (1919-54). His wisdom and learning, so clearly seen in his carefully prepared lectures and the articles he produced for the *Clergy Review*, led him to be described as 'the leading Moral Theologian writing in the English language, and it is no exaggeration to say, one of the leading authorities in the whole Church'. At the time of his death in 1954, a former student recalled that Canon Mahoney was never too busy to see anyone; 'always they were received with politeness, courtesy and patience. The humour that was such a marked feature of his lectures and his writing was not wanting in his ordinary conversation. Many of us must have gone along to see him merely because we wanted him to help us through a period of depression.' He was devoted to teaching and it seems that he begged to be excused from becoming Vicar General and, on another occasion, Auxiliary Bishop. He liked to live simply and, we are told, 'to save time he used to cook seven puddings at once and label them with the names of the days of the week'.

When Fr Moloney arrived at Our Lady of Lourdes the mission covered a large area, including Hillingdon, Ruislip and Eastcote. The growth of population following the extension of the Metropolitan Line from Harrow to Uxbridge in 1904 meant that new parishes needed to be formed. Although others would set up these missions, Fr Moloney had a central role in making the preparations and purchasing land. From as early as 1916 he was looking for a potential site in Ruislip. Four years previously St Vincent's Cripples' Home, run by the Sisters of Charity of St Vincent de Paul, had moved there from Clapham, assuring Ruislip of its first post-Reformation Catholic presence, but what was needed was a more permanent mission. Fr Moloney suggested plots on the Church Croft Estate, on the east side of the High Street, and thanks to the generosity of a local benefactress, Miss Warrender, a church was opened in September 1921, dedicated at her request to the Most Sacred Heart of Jesus.

As the new church was opening at Uxbridge, Fr Moloney was looking for land in Hillingdon. The diocese advised that the new chapel should be within easy access of the Convent of Mercy since 'some of the Nuns who have time to spare could possibly undertake Catechism, cleaning of the Church, etc. It would give some of the old ones something to do.' It was decided to purchase land on Long Lane and commission Mr Scott to design a building that could function as both a school hall and temporary chapel, dedicated to St Bernadette. This was ready to be opened in 1937 and the first priest, Fr Frederick Bentley, initially lived in Woodville Gardens. It was a busy time of Catholic expansion in 'Metroland' for 1937 also saw a new chapel opened at Eastcote, served from Ruislip, while two years later the present church of the Most Sacred Heart was opened on Pembroke Road.

The temporary chapel at Hillingdon, dedicated to St Bernadette

Fr Moloney's health had never been strong and Mgr Carton de Wiart wrote in 1930 that 'he is one of our most devoted priests... At the present moment he is far from well with very high blood pressure and, although he knows that he may drop down dead at any moment, he keeps on doing more than he ought to.' In his final weeks he had been cared for by the Little Company of Mary at Hillingdon Court. Fr Moloney died on St Patrick's Day 1937, aged 65, and his Requiem was celebrated at Uxbridge on 23 March by his close friend Fr Carey of Shepherds Bush, in the presence of Archbishop Hinsley. Afterwards, Fr Moloney was buried at Kensal Green. 'Of him it can be said', wrote the reporter for *The Advertiser and Gazette,* 'that he was a simple kindly man who never said a harsh or unkind word, a man fully imbued with the holiness of his office, and a man who expended his entire energies in the advancement of his work'.

The Gilbey Family of Denham

A plaque in the church memorialises William Crosbie Gilbey and his wife Margarita, who lived at The Lea, Denham. In 1938 two stone statues were placed on either side of the sanctuary in their memory, depicting the Sacred Heart and Our Lady. These were eventually removed in 2002, although the fine statue of the Sacred Heart was located (in a warehouse in Lancashire) and returned to its original plinth in December 2010.

The Gilbeys were great benefactors of the parish and belonged to a well-known family of wine merchants, a business founded by William's father, Alfred, and uncle, Walter. Although William was a partner of the firm, he was keenly interested in fishing and had a hatchery at Denham where he lovingly reared trout. In his history of the House of Gilbey, Alec Waugh recounts how

> his most ambitious venture was an attempt to stock the Thames with salmon. Having heard that Danube salmon did not have to go down to the sea, he felt that this was the fish with which to stock the Thames, where pollution in the lower reaches was such, even then, that no salmon could get through it to spawn. He imported ova from the Danube, hatched them in his Denham hatchery, and put them in the Thames. There is no evidence of success. William's efforts were mocked by *Punch*, with verses including the lines:

>> Down beyond Barking Reach,
>> Foul beyond power of speech,
>> Went the six hundred!

William's wife, Margarita, belonged to the Gordon family of Jerez, themselves wine merchants, and four of their eight children were baptised at Uxbridge: Mercedes (1893), Winifred (1895), Alban (1899) and Marion (1900). Each had multiple baptismal names, all the girls being given 'Maria del Buen Consejo', after Our Lady of Good Counsel. The eldest son, William Gordon Gilbey, lived for many years at The Grove, Denham. He married Grace Mary Eleonor Mostyn, the daughter of Hubert, Seventh Baron Vaux of Harrowden, a title dating back to the reign of Henry VIII. The Barony went into abeyance on Hubert's death in 1935, for there was no male heir, but three years later George VI named Grace as Baroness Vaux of Harrowden. Her new position necessitated the Gilbey family's move to Harrowden, Northamptonshire, but while they lived in Denham, the couple's two sons were baptised at the temporary church on Lawn Road: Peter Hubert (1914) and John Hugh Philip (1915), later respectively the Ninth and Tenth Baron Vaux.

It should be noted that the first of these, Peter Hubert Gilbey, after finishing school at Ampleforth Abbey, decided to stay on as a member of the Benedictine community there, much to his mother's surprise. When she expressed her doubts about his monastic vocation, he told her to consider the feelings of Our Lady at the foot of the cross. He was duly clothed and took the name Gabriel, in view of his great devotion to St Gabriel of Our Lady of Sorrows, the patron saint of students and seminarians. Dom Gabriel was solemnly professed in 1936 and ordained a priest in 1940. When he succeeded his mother as Ninth Baron Vaux in 1958 he became the first Catholic monk to take a seat in the House of Lords since 1559 and when he spoke for the first time in a debate, in 1962, he noted that the last time a monk had addressed the House he was 'confined in a sort of concentration camp for refractory clergy in Wisbech Castle'. Between 1962 and 1976 Dom Gabriel served as parish priest of St Mary's, Warrington, where he was much loved, and died on All Saints Day 1977.

Another well-known clerical member of the family, the nephew of William Crosbie, was Mgr Alfred Newman Gilbey, chaplain to the University of Cambridge for one hundred celebrated terms and described at his death in 1998 as the most widely loved Catholic priest of modern times.

UXBRIDGE AT WAR

FR MOLONEY'S death in 1937 necessitated a new parish priest: Fr Matthew Lynch, originally from Kilmallock, County Limerick, who had most recently been working at New Barnet. According to his obituary in the *Westminster Cathedral Chronicle,* Fr Lynch had to be understood before he could be appreciated: 'outwardly he was often ungracious, outspoken or hesitant, but these were mere signs of supersensitiveness for, beneath the sometimes bluff exterior, there was a heart of gold.' He was particularly noted for his love of the poor and soon after his arrival at Uxbridge it was said by parishioners that 'we see nothing but tramps at the Presbytery since Father Lynch came.' Indeed, 'he helped them daily in many ways and often arranged holidays for them paying the expenses himself. One man who had known better days was once able in this way to spend a month in Paris... Extremely secretive, Fr Lynch was never known to speak of these things himself. He believed in never letting his left hand know what the right was doing.' He was also shrewd and turned away those who abused his charity. On one occasion an undeserving vagrant asked for the fare to Oxford and Fr Lynch replied, 'You're wasting your time. They don't take hobos like you at the University!'

Fr Lynch was known for his ready wit. When a rather pompous parishioner announced that his son was going to a non-Catholic public school 'to get on in the world,' Fr Lynch replied 'Which world?' During his time at New Barnet he joined a committee to care for Belgian refugees at the outbreak of the Great War. 'Turning to Fr Lynch at the first committee meeting, the [non-Catholic] Chairman said, "Their Religion will be cared for by the Rev. Mr Lynch and, I understand, the services will be in Latin. Of course we all know Latin don't we, Mr Lynch?" The reply came like an arrow, *"Utique. Imprimis stultus es!"* (Yes, in the first place you're a fool!) – "Quite, quite," said the bewildered chairman to the great amusement of the non-Catholic Clergy and others who, unlike himself, had fully understood the inference.'

In these pre-ecumenical times, we read that 'it was a practise of Fr Lynch to visit pre-Reformation Protestant Churches in order to bring away as many available drawing pins as possible. When questioned as to the morality of this custom he replies, "That is what we call occult compensation. If the whole Church belongs to us Catholics, who can object to my taking a simple drawing pin or two?" Once, as a joke, but to the horror of the clerical party accompanying him, he threatened to carry off the bambino from a pre-Reformation Church now in the hands of the High Anglicans!'

Fr Lynch shepherded the parish through the troubled times of the Second World War. Uxbridge was, of course, the home of a prominent RAF base and the Battle of Britain was effectively commanded from its underground operations room. The town was bombed during the Blitz, though not to the extent of other parts of London. For example, six were killed on 28 September 1940 when a bomb hit houses on Rockingham Parade, not far from the school. A further four died during the night of 7 November 1940 when ten bombs hit the town, although the casualties could have been much greater since one bomb bounced off the roof of the Savoy cinema, leaving those watching a film inside unharmed. Although the Catholic church survived, that of the Catholic Apostolic Church on Montague Road was destroyed.

The bombing attacks led to changes in all spheres of life, including that of the Church.

Bells were not rung after 16 June 1940 (unless the purpose was 'to give the signal of alarm in case of the approach of parachutists or other air-borne troops') and instructions were issued for said Masses to replace High Masses. A dispensation was granted for people 'to take non-alcoholic liquid nourishment before Holy Communion' (thus breaking the Eucharistic fast) when 'they have to take refuge at night, in time of air-raids' or 'have care of the sick at night'. If the siren sounded while people were in church, priests were given permission to administer general absolution. The black-out disturbed evening services (including such occasions as Midnight Mass) and pastors were told to encourage family prayer at home when they could not meet in church. Nor was the spiritual weapon of prayer ignored - there was a week of prayer and penance in July 1940, for example, including a general Communion and daily prayers of intercession before the Blessed Sacrament. The feast of SS Thomas More and John Fisher fell during this week and Cardinal Hinsley hoped that 'their intercession will protect our beloved land if we have their spirit of Christian fortitude'.

Despite loss of life and the extent of the destruction, the people showed great courage and were united in the 'Blitz Spirit'. Fr Lynch used to hold up his Rosary, saying 'I take my ARP shelter to bed with me,' and we learn that 'his evening stroll would be taken when the gunfire was at its height on the plea that, having bad eyesight, the searchlights helped him to see where he was going.'

The church notice books for the period provide few references to hostilities, though there were weekly prayers for casualties and prisoners-of-war. The Corpus Christi procession of 1944 was arranged '1) to thank Almighty God for the safe deliverance of Rome and of the Holy Father, 2) to beg the blessing of God on our parishioners engaged in the present operations'. In March of the same year there was an appeal for 'voluntary fire watchers for the school' since 'it would be a terrible disaster if our school were gutted by fire in a raid. One unextinguished fire bomb not put out would cause it!'

Fr Lynch experienced great personal sadness in 1940 when he learnt of the death back home in Knocklong of his beloved mother, who he called 'a woman of women.' He built a Lourdes Grotto in her honour at Uxbridge, which stood outside the church until the building of the new hall necessitated its removal, and her death led to a visible breakdown in his own health. As he lay dying in 1944, he often spoke of her and 'during his delirium, he suffered again the agonizing sorrows caused by her death and burial, showing that he never reco-

The Lourdes Grotto
that once stood in the church grounds

vered from the last great sorrow of his life.' Fr Lynch died on the night of 4 September 1944 at St Joseph's Hospice for the Dying at Liverpool. He was 66 years of age and his Requiem was held at Uxbridge on 12 September in the presence of the Archbishop.

Fr Frederick Dixon was appointed parish priest in October 1944. Born in 1895, he was educated at Stamford Hill and St Edmund's, Ware. However, his studies were interrupted by military service with the Honourable Artillery Company in France and Italy during the First World War, during which he was awarded the Military Medal. After the war, he returned to St Edmund's College to prepare for the Priesthood and was ordained in 1923. During the Second World War he was Rector of Bow and showed great courage during the Blitz, during which bombs severely damaged the church, school and presbytery. He probably viewed his move to Uxbridge with some relief.

Perhaps the most colourful of the curates in these years was Fr Joseph Gardner, who went on to found the parish of St Bartholomew, St Albans South in 1959. He wore a monacle, had a small pet dog and was a great sportsman, often taking the schoolchildren to Uxbridge Pool or to Rockingham Recreation Ground for cricket, where he would appear in white flannels and cricket shirt.

**The beginning of a Nuptial Mass at Uxbridge,
c.1962, showing the new marbled apse**

A TIME OF CHANGE

FR DIXON only stayed at Uxbridge four years and in 1948 moved to Osterley, being replaced by Fr John Shaw, who had been ordained (like Fr Dixon) in 1923. Since then, he had worked in the parishes of Kingsland, Gunnersbury, Hillingdon and, most recently, Maiden Lane, where he also served as Diocesan Financial Secretary. His younger brother, Stephen, was also a priest of the diocese and worked for many years as National Director of the Pontifical Mission Aid Societies.

The parish notice books for the late 1940s give a taste of everyday parish life. On Sunday there were three Sunday Masses (8.30, 9.30, 10.30) and an evening service, comprising of rosary, sermon and benediction. Daily Mass was at 7.30 in the morning and, as with any parish, special celebrations punctuated the year – for example, First Holy Communions was the occasion for an all-day exposition of the Blessed Sacrament and a procession in the evening. Several parish groups were organised, including the Knights of St Columba, Children of Mary, Guild of the Blessed Sacrament, the Uxbridge branch of the Westminster Catholic Trade Union Association and a youth club that met at Whitehall School. There was an annual summer fete and regular socials and dances at St Margaret's Hall on Belmont Road to raise money for the school debt. On one occasion it was announced that 'a priest from London has offered to bring a group of kilted children to give an exhibition of dancing'. Whist Drives (and later Football Pools) were also held to raise money, as was a performance of *Cinderella* by a group of parishioners calling themselves the 'Nondescripts' in February 1946.

There were occasional visits from bishops - when Cardinal Bernard Griffin made a visitation in June 1946 the gentlemen of the parish were asked 'to form a Guard of Honour, to line Basset Road on His Eminence's entry to church from house' – and a parish mission in December 1946, conducted by the Redemptorist Fr McNulty.

The summer of 1948 saw the Olympics come to London. Resources were limited in these post-war years and rather than building the usual Olympic Village many male competitors stayed in RAF bases, including Uxbridge. The presbytery seems to have provided accommodation for some of the chaplains, for there is a notice referring to 'our two guest priests, Fr McMahon and Fr English, who were attending to the spiritual needs of the American Olympic members'.

During this period, well-known faces from the silver screen could be sometimes spotted in the congregation, including Finlay Jefferson Currie (who played Abel Magwitch in David Lean's *Great Expectations* and St Peter in *Quo Vadis*), Noel Purcell *(The Blue Lagoon)* and Mary Morris *(The Thief of Baghdad, Pimpernel Smith)*.

'The Merry Canon'

In 1953 Fr Shaw was moved to Fulham and eventually became a Canon of Westminster. He was replaced by another Canon: Bernard Leo St John George. He was born in South Africa on 1 March 1904, his Irish mother having moved there after developing TB. It seems that the sunshine and equitable climate led to a full recovery. Canon George spent his childhood in Wexford and London, where he was educated by the Salesians at Battersea, and worked for a time as a motor insurance salesman. He trained for the Priesthood at St Edmund's, Ware and was ordained in 1934. After serving as curate at Poplar, he was appointed Administrator of the Crusade of Rescue (1948-53).

In 1959 the Canon embarked upon an interesting ecumenical adventure in hiring the Church of England Hall on the High Street, Cowley Peachey, for the celebration of Mass on Sunday mornings. The increasing population of the area necessitated such a Mass Centre and 85 attended the first celebration on 11 October. Canon George commented that it was the feast of the Motherhood of Our Lady and that 'England was once dedicated to Our Lady,

Canon Bernard Leo St John George

and still is for the Faithful, so perhaps the date was not quite accidental'. Around the same time he began looking for a site where a more permanent chapel could be built in Cowley. A piece of suitable land was spotted in Station Road two years later but the reserve price of £30,000 was deemed too expensive. Sunday Mass was celebrated at the hall in Cowley until 1974.

In 1961 Canon George added marble to the apse of the church. It cost around £11,500 and was made possible by his contacts in South Africa. The work caused considerable disruption to church services for several months and Masses were celebrated at the Lady Altar but the result was worth waiting for.

Like his predecessors, the Canon kept a close eye on St Mary's School and saw several generations of children pass through. These included Chris Finnegan, who went on to win a gold medal at the 1968 Olympics as a middleweight boxer and whose funeral would be celebrated at the church in 2009. A particular highlight was the visit of Cardinal Heenan on 8 July 1965; having confirmed seventy children at the church, he was entertained by a concert produced by the pupils. Another episcopal visitor was Bishop Mahon, who came on 7 October 1972 to bless the new Assembly Hall and Kitchens.

The Church and the Town Planners

On 1 July 1929 Fr H. E. G. Rope, a Shrewsbury priest and for many years archivist at the English College, Rome, made a rather eccentric journey from Oxford to London by means of a 'Tally-ho Coach' with 'four splendid horses in the finest condition, the guard in beaver hat and scarlet coat' and the driver 'wearing the grey top hat and long frock-coat of mid-Victorian days.' Fr Rope published an account of his experience and noted that 'Uxbridge itself has still some local characteristics, but one trembles for its narrow streets, doomed, no doubt, to be widened for the "boiler-bounder" who coolly "demands" the extermination of all good things to gratify his savage greed of pace'.

Cardinal Heenan processing into the church

68

Fr Rope was right to predict that the old streets of Uxbridge would soon fall into the hands of developers. It was felt that the High Street was often clogged up with traffic, land in prime locations underused and some of the older buildings were clearly in a poor state of preservation. Drastic proposals for the redevelopment of the town centre were produced over several years and finally approved in 1965, with an emphasis on shopping facilities, parking and a relief road to divert traffic from the High Street. Unfortunately it meant the destruction of picturesque Cross Street (with its timber-framed buildings), the gardens of the Cedars (the old home of the Fassnidge family) and much of Basset Road, Lawn Road and the Lynch. Uxbridge would remain an important commercial centre but lost much of its character as an 'old world English market town', with its family businesses and venerable public houses.

Proposals were made to relocate Our Lady of Lourdes and St Michael and several sites were offered, including Belmont Road (where Christ Church was later built) and the former station on Vine Street (near Randalls). There was even a suggestion that the church could be moved brick-by-brick and rebuilt. However, Canon George was adamant that the church should remain where it had stood for so many decades.

The existing site was, after all, well-placed for the town centre and St Mary's school and, having just painstakingly added marble to the sanctuary, the Canon had no wish to build a new church. The building could surely continue to serve the Catholic community in the future, he thought, especially if a parish hall was built. However, the redevelopment of Uxbridge meant that the church became isolated on a virtual traffic island and even today there are probably many locals who are unaware of its existence.

A parish hall had long been a dream – indeed, as early as 1929, the Archbishop had suggested the building of a parish centre that could double up as a church until a more permanent building was erected. After the opening of the new church in 1931, the need for a hall was strongly felt and in 1961 the parish tried to secure land for this purpose, although planning permission was turned down since it was 'premature to the Uxbridge Town Centre Redevelopment'. However, the Canon hoped that the new plans for the town might allow for improved church precincts and space for an ample hall. Since the only piece of vacant land belonging to the parish was to be swallowed up by the new relief road – the subject of a compulsory purchase order - negotiations were soon made for an exchange of lands so that a parish centre could be built at the side of the church. Various plans were considered, including the demolition of the presbytery so that a three storey structure could be built, with a parish club and, on the top floor, living space for the clergy. However, the design proved to be too costly and subsequent parish priests can be thankful that this was never realised, for the rather cramped clergy living quarters would have been directly above the parish club and bar!

A cheaper option was to erect a prefabricated structure that could be built quickly and eventually be replaced by something more permanent. However, there were all sorts of bureaucratic and logistical delays and the more ambitious plans were thwarted by the presence of important cables and pipes underground. By June 1973 there had been 23 meetings with Council officials and 92 letters written by the parish architect alone.

Living in the midst of a major building site caused much stress for the incumbents of the presbytery on what was now renamed Osborn Road. The church buildings became affected by dust and splashed with mud, while the brickwork was damaged by heavy vehicles and nearby demolitions; even the church interior deteriorated by the accumulation of mud and debris outside. Heaps of excavated material surrounded the presbytery and the construction workers often used the priests' front garden to navigate round these obstacles. Access to the church became restricted and there was even less parking space than usual on Sunday. One parishioner even wrote to the Town Clerk suggesting that trees and grass be planted in front of the presbytery as 'a courteous and kindly gesture of sympathy for the parish priest and his household, who have carried out their duties so uncomplainingly under the trying circumstances of demolition and reconstruction'.

Canon George retired in 1974, still with no hall built. He remained in the area, living in the newly-erected Fairlie House and acting as a supply priest to the parish. He died on 18 December 1980, aged 76, and was buried at Hillingdon Cemetery after a Requiem Mass at the Cathedral. His one-time assistant, Fr Michael Moriarty, said at the time that 'one could write volumes on that lovely priest, with his boyish pranks and harmless practical jokes. He would be full of concern if he ever thought he had done an injustice to anybody'.

The new parish priest was Fr Andrew Clancy, originally from County Clare, who had served as an army chaplain and saw service in India, Burma and Malaya. Having worked for many years in the diocese of Beauvais, he had most recently served as parish priest of St George's, Sudbury. Fr Clancy remained in Uxbridge a short time and was replaced after two years by Fr John Dutton, an energetic priest with a great passion for youth work. Both priests continued to work towards gaining planning

**The presbytery at the time
of the town redevelopment.**

permission for the new parish hall. The idea of a two storey building with general purpose hall, kitchen, office, club rooms, bar and accommodation for two priests and a housekeeper was considered. Planning permission was granted for a simpler design in 1975 but once again nothing came of it. It was left to the fourth priest to be involved in the project, Fr Trnka, to oversee its completion.

A Czech Refugee

Fr Oldrich Joseph Trnka arrived in Uxbridge in 1978. Born in the Czech town of Pilsen, he wrote a short memoir of his life on the occasion of his golden jubilee of ordination:

> I always wanted to be a priest. My first recollection is of a pilgrimage to the shrine of Our Lady on the Holy Mountain, forty miles from our home town. When we got there, an old priest took notice of the little boy I was then and brought the miraculous statue down to me at the altar rails. He touched my forehead with it and blessed me. I felt a great longing to be like him. In our home parish we had a Dominican Fathers and they meant everything to me. I was their altar boy and one evening during the Exposition of the Blessed Sacrament I realized that more than the profusion of flowers, of the candle lights and incense, it was the Lord Jesus who was there, and that my whole

future was to be with him as his priest in his Presence.

Oldrich joined the Dominicans, took the religious name 'Konstanc' and was ordained on 29 June 1938, just as war clouds were looming. He was arrested by the Gestapo in 1942 and spent some time at a concentration camp, but he managed to regain his freedom and discreetly taught Greek and Latin in a Czech village and celebrate Mass in people's houses. As he later recalled, things did not get better with peace:

> In 1945 the war ended, but the evil of the war was not atoned for and we wondered what was going to happen next. We did not have to wait long before we saw the Stalinists taking over the liberated countries one after another. Central and Eastern Europe lost their freedom and the Church of the faithful fell under the power of the worst enemy of all times. The plan to destroy the Church was put into operation and all priests were pressurised into giving up their vocation or collaborating with the regime. The penalties for non-cooperation were merciless and harsh. Hundreds of priests were taken away from their parishes or religious houses and put into prisons, sent to work underground, unprotected from radiation and dangerous chemicals, or killed after torture. Some were just forbidden to officiate as priests and given menial jobs to go to. I was

to be a labourer in a steel mill, but I refused and continued my priest's work as before. I was thinking of St Peter who after his arrest said, "We must obey God rather than men", and of St Paul of whom the Lord Jesus said, "I myself will show him how much he will have to suffer for my sake". By now our people were getting frightened and many stopped seeing me. Then one night a courageous, friendly policeman came quickly to tell me that my arrest was imminent. My bag was packed and I slipped away. If I could reach the border 200 miles away and cross into the American Zone in Germany, I would be free. I alerted two of my friends and together we decided to risk it.

As we were crossing the mountainous border area, we were spotted by heavily armed border guards. We thoughùt this was the end and were just about to give ourselves up when – the earth opened under our feet and we fell into a ditch just big enough to hide us. Long grass bent over the opening and we could be seen no more. We felt terribly grateful, as if angels themselves were looking after us, and kept very quiet. When we finally ventured out the guards had gone and during the night we managed to cross the border. We became refugees. A US Army truck took us to a refugee camp and there we stayed on looking for a new home somewhere in the free world. I went to Switzerland but they did not want refugee priests there. I worked in a factory and after two years, thanks to the intervention of a friendly anglican bishop, I came to England. When the ferry was approaching the cliffs of Dover I felt a great urge to pray for and bless the people of this island.

The first few years of exile were spent in Switzerland, where he worked in a timber yard and studied theology at the University of Basel. In 1952 he came to England for a language course, only intending to stay for six weeks: 'I never wanted to live in England. All I knew about it was the cigarettes and the wonderful breakfasts,' he told a local reporter on his arrival at Uxbridge, 'I really wanted to go to America'. He was naturalised in 1958 and, after working in several south London parishes, incardinated into the diocese of Westminster in 1970. Before coming to Uxbridge he had worked for nearly eight years as a chaplain at the Cathedral and had charge of Sacred Heart, Horseferry Road.

Fr Trnka quickly settled into life in Uxbridge. He is remembered as a devout priest, often seen praying in the church and strict about behaviour during Mass – 'on leaving the church after Mass', one parishioner wrote, 'any miscreants were quietly admonished in a discreet but firm, courteous and almost jocular manner but without giving offence'. His newsletters were devotional and uplifting and he had a great love for Our Lady.

At long last, the parish saw the completion of the hall at the side of the presbytery and church. On Fr Trnka's arrival, just £19,000 had been saved for this purpose and this was nearly doubled through a concentrated period of special collections and fund-raising events. Helped by a loan from the diocese, construction began at the end of 1982 and was ready the following April, though it was not formally opened (by Bishop Mahon) until July. Fr Trnka told the local *Gazette* that 'the parish has been waiting more than 50 years for this hall'.

Shortly afterwards, in 1983, Fr Trnka was transferred to the parish of Cranford. He retired in 1990 but, despite crippling arthritis, worked at the Czech Chapel, Farm Street and died in January 2003, his Requiem being celebrated at Uxbridge by Bishop George Stack. He was buried in the same grave as Canon George at Hillingdon Cemetery.

His successor was Fr Horatio Hosford, a kind man who is remembered for his dogs and his repertoire of funny stories. He was a good listener and shrewd in dealing with people's problems; he reminded one parishioner of Barry Fitzgerald, who played Fr Fitzgibbon in the film *Going My Way*. Many attended a special Mass on 23 May 1984 to celebrate his silver jubilee of ordination.

SCHOOLS
AND CONVENTS

THE HISTORY of Catholicism in Uxbridge does not only comprise of the parish church and St Mary's School. Over the years there were other institutions in the locality that should be briefly mentioned.

Pield Heath Convent and School

The English Province of the Sisters of the Sacred Hearts of Jesus and Mary opened a residential Special School at Pield Heath House in 1901, at the invitation of Cardinal Vaughan – one of the first such schools in the country. The community had originally come to London as a small group of refugees in search of safety following the outbreak of the Franco-Prussian War in 1870 and initially settled in the Stratford area, working among the poor of the East End. They subsequently made foundations in Scotland and Wales, teaching in Poor Law schools, nursing in cottage hospitals and helping in the rehabilitation of young street girls as well as providing homes for single mothers and their babies. In 1903, on the advice of Cardinal Vaughan, most of the sisters of the English Province opted to form a separate congregation, with the motherhouse in Chigwell in Essex. Today the so-called 'Chigwell Sisters' also have missions in various parts of the UK, Ireland, California, El Salvador, Zambia, Uganda and the Philippines.

In December 1900, Cardinal Vaughan met with Sr Winifride Tyrell, the Provincial, and invited her to open a residential school for 'feeble-minded children' in the diocese. The Pield Heath school opened on 5 January 1901 with 15 pupils. The following year the school was certified by the Board of Education for 62 boys and girls and a new wing was added in 1908. Then in 1911 the boys re-located to Ormskirk in Lancashire and Pield Heath became a girls only school until the 1980s.

On the feast of St Edward the Confessor 1923 Cardinal Bourne opened a new chapel and infirmary, on which occasion Fr Moloney celebrated High Mass and the Cardinal gave an address afterwards. It was consecrated on 5 November 1931 by Bishop Butt. Pield Heath was for many years an important Mass Centre for that part of the parish. In February 1988 Cardinal Hume opened Marian House next to the school, on Kingston Lane, which goes from strength to strength as a nursing home for elderly sisters, with a resident chaplain.

In November 1993 Diana, Princess of Wales paid a visit to the school. Due to the sudden flurry of the media who also attended that day (following the publication of an intrusive picture of the Princess at her London gym), Diana asked to return on a private visit. This took place on the day of the children's Christmas lunch later that year, which the Princess heartily enjoyed, together with Princes William and Harry.

Pield Heath is still a flourishing school for children and young people with complex learning needs and associated communication difficulties. Pupils range between the ages of 7 and 19. Pield Heath School, which also offers residential and respite care, deals with nineteen local authorities including many London boroughs. In 2010 OFSTED rated the school as 'outstanding' for the second time.

Rockingham House School

In 1907 St James' Catholic Preparatory School for Young Gentleman, under the direction of

Miss Mary Julia Butt, was moved from Baylis House, Slough to Rockingham House, Uxbridge, a stone's throw from the parish school. St James' had been founded in 1823 by two convert brothers, William Henry and James Palmer Butt, and moved to Slough seven years later. For long it was the only Catholic school in the locality and provided one of only two Catholic chapels in the whole of Buckinghamshire. Indeed, the mission at Slough had been founded by the school chaplain in 1885. Baylis House numbered among its alumni the future Cardinal Rafael Merry del Val (Secretary of State to St Pius X), Archbishop Joseph Butt (an auxiliary in Westminster and a member of the family that ran the school) and Bishop William Keatinge (the first Bishop to the Forces). However, by the time the school moved to Uxbridge the glory days were over and it faced bankruptcy. A contemporary advert stated that 'the oldest Catholic Preparatory School in England has always offered to boys from four to thirteen years of age a thorough grounding in solid religious principles, and in all the ordinary subjects of an up-to-date education, thus preparing boys for the Catholic Colleges. Assiduous care is bestowed upon the health and welfare of the boys. School games are played on the premises under supervision. Entire charge is taken of boys whose parents live abroad, and to whom inclusive fees are offered'.

During the school's sojourn in Uxbridge, it became closely involved in parish life. In the summer of 1918, for example, a garden fete was held in the school grounds 'in aid of the funds of the Church of Our Lady of Lourdes', where 'in the shade of the trees, stalls were attractively set, together with all sorts of novel competitions and games to bring in the money', including Belgian Confiserie, hoop-la, ninepins, 'bursting the balloons' and a most successful 'open-air whist drive'. Entertainment was provided by the Uxbridge and Hillingdon Band and 'in the evening the Gadabouts, an entertaining party of ladies from Hayes, gave a nice performance'. It must have provided a welcome distraction from the horrors of war and, as one might expect at such a time, the community pulled together. In thanking Mr G. E. Smith, J. P. for opening the fete, Fr Moloney 'spoke with pleasure upon the help received from people outside the Catholic Church'. Unfortunately, the school did not stay long at Rockingham House and in 1920 moved to Milford House, Windsor Road, Slough. It was finally closed down ten years later.

'Blue Nuns' at Hillingdon Court

In 1923 the Little Company of Mary (often known as the 'Blue Nuns') moved from Gunnersbury House, Hounslow to Hillingdon Court, near Uxbridge – 'a beautiful nursing and convalescent home, surrounded by nine acres of magnificent grounds'. It was formally opened by Cardinal Bourne on 8 May 1923: 'the beautiful grounds are now at their best, and the visitors greatly enjoyed a stroll round them. Tea was served on the lawn. The entire convent was thrown open for the inspection of visitors, as, the day being so fine, the greater number of the patients were able to be enjoying the sunshine in the garden.' Benediction was given and a telegram received from Cardinal Gasparri, conveying the Pope's blessing. The Order had been founded by Mary Potter in Nottingham in 1877 and approved by Leo XIII in 1893. As has already been mentioned, the sisters cared for Fr Moloney in his last days. The nursing home later transferred to Sudbury Hill, Harrow.

Sisters of Mercy at The Knoll

The Sisters of Mercy moved to The Knoll, Court Drive, Hillingdon in 1925, when it was still part of the Uxbridge parish. Their house was dedicated to St Raphael and the location (surrounded by park land) a great contrast to their convent in Commercial Road, from which they came. The house had been donated to Cardinal Bourne by Mrs Lacon Gordon and was officially opened in August 1926. It acted as a rest home for sisters who needed refuge from the slums of the east end. During the Second World War many of the sisters were evacuated to Hillingdon.

Bridgettines at Iver Heath

Finally, mention should be made of the Bridgettines of Iver Heath, who are occasional visitors to the church, even though their community lives outside the parish and, indeed, just across the diocesan boundary. Their convent was founded in 1931, when five sisters

The chapel of the Blue Nuns at Hillingdon Court

were sent to the Buckinghamshire village by Blessed Elizabeth Hesselblad. They settled in an impressive Tudor-style house on Fulmer Common Road and opened a house of prayer and hospitality, still used today by groups and those wanting a place to stay within easy reach of Pinewood Studios and Heathrow. Interestingly, the first superior of the Iver Heath convent, Catherine Flanagan, has had her cause for beatification opened. As already mentioned, this was not the first Bridgettine presence in the area for part of the Syon community found shelter at Denham after the dissolution of their abbey in the 1530s.

INTO THE
THIRD MILLENNIUM

FROM 1994 to 2004 the parish was guided by Fr Colin Whatling, a Yorkshireman who had seen service in the Royal Navy in his youth. Much work was done to the church premises: the back of the church was restructured (creating a room for restless children), the roof recovered and disabled access provided with the ramp at the west front. The Lady Altar was also renovated and the sanctuary re-ordered – the new marble altar was dedicated by Bishop George Stack (later Archbishop of Cardiff) on 23 June 2002.

In an effort to highlight the church's presence in the town, Fr Whatling put up a large sign in papal colours facing oncoming traffic, especially for visitors who would otherwise drive past without seeing the building. Like many other parishes in the diocese, Uxbridge participated in the 'At Your Word Lord' programme of renewal and the tradition of organising regular 'small community faith sharing groups' was started.

Fr Matthew Heslin arrived in the autumn of 2004 and undertook major building work in the presbytery, which by this time was in need of repair. He also renovated the church floor (much to his delight), negotiated with the Council over parking restrictions around the church and led pilgrimages to Lourdes and Aylesford. In 2008, to mark the 150th anniversary of the apparitions at Lourdes, a successful Dinner Dance was organised by the parish at Brunel University.

In September 2009 Fr Heslin was moved down the road to Hillingdon and Fr Nicholas Schofield appointed in his place. He combined his duties as parish priest with work as diocesan archivist. A Friday Holy Hour was started, initially as part of the 'Year for Priests', and in March 2010 Fr John Edwards SJ led a week-long Parish Mission, at which there was an average daily attendance of about a hundred. Further highlights were provided by parish pilgrimages to Walsingham and Rome and the State Visit of Pope Benedict XVI in September 2010 – sizeable parish groups attended both the prayer vigil at Hyde Park and the beatification of Cardinal Newman in Birmingham.

For the seventy-fifth anniversary of the church's consecration and eightieth anniversary of its opening, Archbishop Vincent Nichols celebrated a Solemn Mass on 15 May 2011, attended by the local MP and Mayor, and several hundred parishioners.

Fr Heslin's farewell party 29 September 2009
Fr Schofield (left) Fr Heslin (right)

Here the author, who happens to be the current parish priest, must lay aside his pen and wait for another to continue the story. It is always humbling to acknowledge the debt we owe to past generations. We think not only of priests and religious but the many parishioners who tirelessly (and often very quietly) worked behind the scenes to build up God's Kingdom in Uxbridge. No parish could function without servers and other ministers, sacristans, musicians, flower arrangers, cleaners, handy-men, secretaries and housekeepers (like the redoubtable Mrs Vedova). The community could not flourish without the many organisations and institutions that have existed over the years and those who helped organise social events and fund raising campaigns. The faith could not have been effectively passed on without the efforts of teachers and catechists – and here we should mention, amongst others, Pauline Fahy who worked for several years as pastoral assistant until her untimely death in 2007. The names of many of these individuals may not be recorded for posterity but their names are known to God and to those they have touched. This little book is as much a tribute to them as to past parish priests!

Visitors are sometimes taken aback by the church's location, situated as it is between a shopping centre and a busy dual carriageway.

However, its presence amidst the hustle and bustle of modern life is eloquent testimony to the place of the Church in the heart of the world. Our Lady of Lourdes and St Michael manages to be an oasis of peace and the beating heart of a vibrant community. In recent years, the parish had benefitted from an explosion in the Catholic population, including the welcome presence of many ethnic groups – whereas in October 2000 the average Sunday Mass attendance was 415, by October 2010 it was just under 600. With the potential redevelopment of the former RAF Uxbridge, this trend is set to continue.

As the church celebrated its eightieth year, a parish profile in the diocesan newspaper *(Westminster Record)* noted that 'the church is in the style of a Roman basilica. Once inside, this architectural style makes it possible for the imagination to transform the asphalt highway outside into Rome's river Tiber and the church into one of the churches on its banks. There certainly is the same sense of eternity.' May this sense of God's presence continue for many years to come.

A LIST OF
UXBRIDGE CLERGY

Rectors and Parish Priests of Uxbridge

1892	Fr Michael Aloysius Wren
1896	Fr James J. Hazell
1897	Fr John Brady
1915	Fr Thomas Moloney
1937	Fr Matthew Lynch
1944	Fr Frederick Dixon
1948	Fr John B. Shaw
1953	Canon Bernard Leo George
1973	Fr Andrew Clancy
1976	Fr John Dutton
1978	Fr Oldrich Trnka
1983	Fr Horatio Hosford
1994	Fr Colin Whatling
2004	Fr Matthew Heslin
2009	Fr Nicholas Schofield

Assistant Priests

Fr John Joseph Wren (1892-95)
Fr Lionel Goodrich (1895-96)
Fr Wilfrid G. Thompson (1896-97)
Fr David Coghlan (1909-11)
Fr William W. Leonard (1911-12)
Fr Thomas Lloyd (1912-14)
Fr Patrick Kelly (1914-15)
Fr Edward Mahoney (1915-17)
Fr Walter Ormiston (1931-37)
Fr Albert Davey (1936-37, 39-46)
Fr Joseph Gardner (1937-46)
Fr Leonard Collingwood (1946-47)
Fr Peter Needham (1947-51)
Fr Leslie Cole (1951-53)
Fr Michael J. Moriarty (1953-63)
Fr James McCormick (1963-66)
Fr James Whitehead (1967-73)

SOURCES USED

Westminster Diocesan Archives

Letter Books of Mgr Carton de Wiart,
Financial Secretary

Parish Archives

Notice books, Correspondence,
Newspaper cuttings, Photos

Books and Journals

The Tablet

The Edmundian

Westminster Cathedral Chronicle

BROWNLOW, F. W. *Shakespeare,
Harsnett and the Devils of Denham* (1993)

CARAMAN, Philip *John Gerard,
The Autobiography of an Elizabethan* (1951)

CARAMAN, Philip *William Weston* (1955)

CARAMAN, Philip
Henry Garnet and the Gunpowder Plot
(1964)

COTTON, Carolynne *Uxbridge Past* (1994)

DE SALIS, Rachel
Hillingdon Through Eleven Centuries
(1926)

DUFFY, Eamon *Fires of Faith:*
Catholic England under Mary Tudor
(2009)

KELLY, Bernard *Historical Notes*
on English Catholic Missions (1907)

PEARCE, Ken *A Century of Uxbridge* (2007)

PEARCE, Ken *Cowley Through Time* (2010)

ROPE, H. E. G.
Forgotten England and Other Musings
(1931)

SIMPSON, Richard *Edmund Campion*
1896)

SKINNER, James *Histories of St Mary's School,*
Uxbridge & St Catherine's, West Drayton
(privately published)

SKINNER, James *Around Uxbridge* (2004)

WAUGH, Alec *Merchants of Wine,*
Being a Centenary Account of the House
of Gilbey (1957)